I0825438

IF I HAD SAID BEAUTY

poems

TAMI HAALAND

Author Photo by Michael North
Cover Art: "Recalling," by Rowene Weems, a photograph with post-processing, pastels and colored pencils
Book Design: Christine Lysnewycz Holbert

FIRST EDITION

This and other fine LOST HORSE PRESS titles may be purchased online at www.losthorsepress.org.

Library of Congress Cataloging-in-Publication Data may be obtained directly from the Library of Congress.

ISBN 979-8-9890965-8-9

for the ancestors
known and unknown
my gratitude

CONTENTS

I

II

III

I am out with lanterns, looking for myself.

—Emily Dickinson
Letter to Elizabeth Holland

My longing is not my own.
It is just as old as the stars.

—Par Lagerkvist
Evening Land

PRELUDE

Listen. I choose this self in the absence of any other for whom I can speak. Call it selfish, this I, a window out, a door, a quirk of time and space, a place for a little while before it dissolves into constituent elements and becomes reinvented as insect, rabbit, tree, soil, however it goes.

The soul, the spirit—how do you tell them apart? The source of words and ideas continues, I believe, though like anyone I have no tangible proof. Do I say I? Only because of what is possible.

The lines leading to this body, mostly Scandinavian, then British, Irish, German, with a certain percentage of many peoples, Neanderthal, and Homo whoever whose remnants we cannot trace. The lines go deeper, become invisible, lead everywhere and nowhere, to molecules, to the sea.

(WHEN THEY SAY) KNOW THYSELF

That day, standing outside
the music room playing
a racing game with classmates
you made fun of the girl
who would be first to die
among you. And your
teacher heard how petty
you were and spoke
to show you this was not
your best self. Still you persist,
discontent shadow
of who you want to be.

Who do you want to be,
dear shadow, and how to
persist? Your best self
searching for words, for
wonder, your teacher
the world and you the girl
racing with the others
for the joy of wind
and speed, the body
your vehicle, and you
far beyond the music room
still standing outside.

SELF-PORTRAIT WITH MITOCHONDRIAL DNA

From the early *L3* who came out of Africa or went deeper in. From *N* who went into the Balkans, Russia, Eastern Europe, then *U* and *K1*, with three of the four subtypes tied to the earliest of Ashkenazi Jews, which puts our line in the Levant, maybe, and *A*, which connects to millions who nurtured our relations, who are distant cousins. We are 1 to 4 percent Neanderthal, those peaceful ones, I like to think, who played flute and made prayers 60,000 years ago. Maybe one ancestor was conceived near fire on animal skins, maybe a cave for shelter, maybe spring.

In the elevator between the lobby and fifth floor of an unfamiliar building, I panic. What if mother's mitochondria, my grandmother's and great grandmother's back to our Eve—who carried the most recent mutation, say 28,000 years ago who passed to her children a replica of her own DNA—what if I am the end of her line, my brothers passing on Y's, me sending mitochondria into my sons? A terrible responsibility I didn't know I had, but then I remember the science, these many relations and my girl cousins, born to my aunt, their daughters and granddaughters, energetic mitochondria of the cell moving forward.

We come from early hunters, Central Asian nomads, Ice Age ancestors who wintered in North Africa. Maybe they are still here for some of us, an impulse or gesture, midnight appetite, a craving for crisp fruit. We've tracked animals, made tools, built fires. We are diggers, caretakers, talkers, travelers, keepers of stories. More than a few of us have envied the flight of birds.

ANOTHER

She's the one who could have been, my
flip side who shows herself in single
strands of black or red hair, a longer lash.
In my brown eye a bit of hazel,
a slip of green. Her skin more olive, and her
hair—our mother would have loved
the curls. This other self is taller.
She may be more serious, more fluid
in public, more athletic, a singer
without perfect pitch, maybe less patient
or more, my recessive/dominant other,
the one who was never expressed, only now
and then a hint: these gray strands below
my temple, their waves signaling our potential.

WHEN I FLY TO EUROPE

I admire the stewards who are taller
than I am, a slightly different gene pool.
At health checks, I sometimes come up short,
but if I remember to stretch and
elongate my spine, the result is better.

We are from our people, their migrations
and landings. Our composition–

that's another question. Seventy or
eighty percent lean muscle mass, twenty
or thirty percent fat. Or another way, maybe
three percent bacteria by volume. And if we
think of water, sixty percent or more.

If not for bodies, we might be streams
plunging from sharp ledges to dark pools.

ENTANGLEMENT

Think of the travelers, how they shed
hair and cells, leave microscopic
particles in seat cushions, in air.

How their bacteria migrate
from person to person, hurting
or helping—this great dispersal.

Consider how saliva on envelopes
sails the world. Even if you are
alone, things come to you.

How can we not get along?
We are everywhere, among each other,
already mixed and woven.

Bombs or drones or suicide vests,
bigotry or bulldozers through wetlands—
nothing can stop this mingling.

HOW LIGHT DISPERSES

Flying over the Great Lakes, I see land shelved
down to darkness, then a peninsula and in it,
more lakes as deep, it seems, as the ocean.
To navigate around water instead of pray
for rain, to see water in the foreground so the mind
has no need to imagine it in the distance
or the future. Given water, the eye perceives
how sun lays down a path on its surface,
and from that bright center, how light
disperses outward into waves and disappears.

An artist explains how, in Monet's haystack, light
removes itself into dim shadows below, explains
how he layered paint from a lightning bolt and
blended colors outward to the night sky.

The lightning is not the painting, nor
the sun's reflection a lake or an ocean.
First the water, its surface woven in paths of wave
and current, the implied swift-moving scale
and gill, tooth and spine, briny stars and crabs
before they wash to shore. First the sky, grey blue
and ominous before the crack, the flash.
First the prairie, whose iridescent green beetles,
larkspur and shrunken lupine anticipate rain.

BAT AT NOON

The swoop, skim, rise and slip over water,
almost bird-like. No coast, no glide.

A gulp of insect and up the craggy
cottonwood bark to a bat-sized crevice,

perfect place in the shadowy daylight
of late, late summer. We face each other.

How good to meet you, I say. It clicks
beyond the ragged bark into the space

between us, quick pulses of sonar
to find and map the other. It is

learning, as I am. It is a vague contour,
and I cannot see its skin, its slight fingers,

the fine-veined texture of its wings.
What allows me to feel how it

huddles in the crevice, looking down?
When I step away, it clicks again, and

I return to this conversation—if it is
a conversation. *I see you,* I say,

then listen through moist summer heat
for its barely audible reply.

FLICKER BUILDS A NEST

beneath a branch in the dying
willow to keep rain from her door.
Ear to bark, I hear her rough out
walls, a pile of woodchips at my feet.
By June, I assume children.

Later her crazy calls echo
in the kitchen, and I go out to see
a cat climbing. Whenever she calls,
I walk the fence with a long stick
and poke until the cat retreats.

One day she calls when a sharp-shinned
hawk guts a robin in the elm. Feathers
on grass show where he was plucked
from the air. Torn between flicker and
hawk, I choose to chase the hawk away.

Days later, she urges her single child
to follow her tree to tree and up the street
until I no longer hear what they say.

THE EDGE OF THINGS

From childhood I wondered—
the line between here
and not here, long division
into the slim margin between.
Couldn't anything be halved,
an instant broken?

The shore is higher this spring,
water over reeds and cattails,
pools in prairie grass. Geese
crouch near the ragged
border, trails submerged.
Where is an edge that is true?

A cliff maybe, a clean
fall, but the falling divisible,
a split and wounded passage.
My quarrel with time and space,
a line where ceiling and
wall converge. Edge

of a cloud, a person.
Childhood lessons in yes/no
a misconception. How
solid could memory be,
how pliant? How far
must we go to be gone?

BONE SELF

This morning I visit an aging friend, her eye
sockets barely covered with skin. Scaffolding,
her underlying truth. From the dental chair
a panoramic view of my skeletal jaw
lit from behind. I feel bones, believe in bones
but fail to see them unless x-rays or some
other force reveals what's underneath. A fall
from a horse, for example, a compound fracture
piercing skin, or a soldier ordered into a trench
during a nuclear test. When the bomb exploded,
he could see the bones of his arms and fingers
though his eyes were closed. And meanwhile,
we trust bones to give form, proportion,
persist as hangers for muscle and skin.
When we say *on the inside,* we don't mean bone.

MAPLE AND LACE

The room is static, cool morning air,
a single lamp. If not for the barely
audible bell tones in her ears, there is
silence and sometimes the sound
of wind in the chimney, the sensation
of a heartbeat. Once she read
ringing in the right ear means
an angel is near, but for her
it is the ghosts who cloy and vanish,
their stories, their histories weaving
the air. She hopes they are secure
in their afterlives but how close
might that be. An inhale, a glance.
It is her job to remember and
discover. So many names.
In time she too will blend
into the forgotten past. But now
the heart beats, the breath works
as it has since the beginning of lungs.

ORDINARY DAY

This morning I find myself in a long
conversation about omens. The woman
who visits at lunchtime sees angels
in her dream. They give her water,
shine lights, but it is not my dream to tell.

Tonight, a friend describes a haunted
library, haunted towns, ghosts in bed
with visitors, the usual steps in hallways,
doors opening, windows closing.
I learn ghosts can follow you home.

My friend says it's best to open
the doors, tell the ghost *you can't*
stay here anymore. Simple as talking
to the living when you've had enough.

PROLEGOMENA

Because I was struck early by the fact
of their leaving, their departures connected
to my own breath, before I knew how my lungs
and heart would continue in their absence.
Because few are left to tell the stories
attached to inherited pieces and portraits,
I go searching for traits of the living
in ghosts, shadows of their words in my sons
or myself. We would not be if not for these
lives and the monuments they made. Because
I am not content with reduction to a few
generations, a simple story of origins.
Because we are from far off continents,
from a long time ago, from both sides
of wars and borders and fences, killers and killed.

II

ORG CHART OF THE SELF

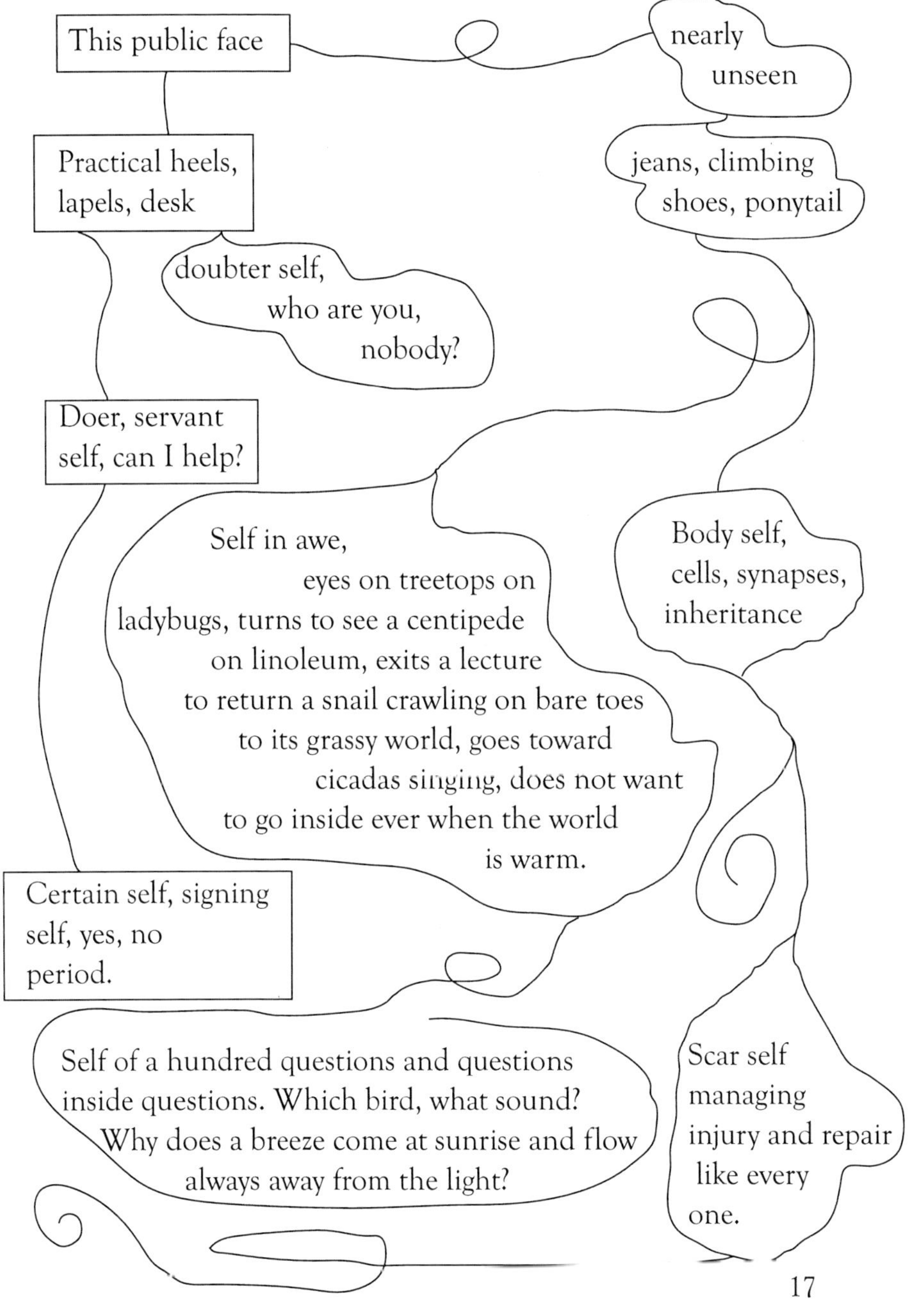

UNDERSTANDING SILENCE

Words didn't do. She angled one way
and another. Sentences couldn't complete.
It was awkward, this—was it a feeling?
This choked voice. Her strength:
invisibility. A friend said maybe
some archetype, some churning
in the gut welling up, something
old. Now and then she had it, a firefly,
a flash, then nothing. It would come
her friend said. It would arrive
without words, silence a part
of the invisible. What if
it was so old it was not yet human,
what if it was old human, inherited
memory. Except for nomadic
tendencies and a host of animals
now extinct on the horizon,
wouldn't much of it have been
the same? Who was it, in that time?
Who was it who said, now
you must speak?

FLY IN WINTER

A speck of a fly bothers itself around me,
crawls on my computer screen. It makes
no sound, doesn't bite and I wonder
if it's lonely, if it senses a body no matter
the size and makes do. Yesterday I took
a swing, monster of me against its dodgy
helplessness. Today, it sails in and out
of my sight. Where it goes, I don't know.
How it knows to reappear is beyond me.
What's the point in killing a single
tiny fly? If it means to trouble my nostrils
or consider a nip, it seems half-hearted,
as tired of winter as I am, as sheltered
inside as the spider who makes her home
in the corner where I never dust. I think
it might like me. When I walk to another
room, it follows. Though its lifespan might
have run out, I think I see it sometimes,
more fleeting before it disappears.

VISITATION

Skin of my arm in a sheen of sweat,
a landing for flies and mosquitos.

I admire their shine, their brilliant
nattering, and welcome a butterfly,

orange ephemera flitting and returning,
settling into the shade of my camera.

It may be disappointed I am not
a flower, my only nectar salt,

but it stays, its wings languid until
I disrupt the scene to walk farther

and take a turn to the river where
I come upon a colony of orange

camouflaged in gravel and breeze, wings
pulsing, so the surface is never still.

A CIRCLE, A WORLD

1

I know some branches have not yet leafed out,
mummified berries from Mountain Ash
have nearly disappeared and the tree

has gone to full flower this year. Beside it, a history
of juniper, news of pansies and petunias.
A society of ponderosa and spruce.

2

You are nearly I, you speak to the self, what is certain
and indefinite. You set your morning shoes against
the deck rail. You are the changeable

body, a location. You are here and wandering,
perplexed in the desire to know.

3

But *you* sit inside at the computer. I hear you
through the screen. You clear your throat. You have
little and much to say. We are a habit

of introversion. We are a pattern on repeat,
a kaleidoscopic turning.

4

They are the grown children beside us who are
also us when we expand the circle one layer.
Then another layer to include parents,

siblings, cousins, neighbors. They also say I and you. We
intersect, we meld, ancestors and far distant
relations through time, exponential circles,

an expanding sculpture—how useless to make
hard lines of division, to blow up a circle, a world.

THE MIND LAYS BY ITS TROUBLE

Light filters through windows in a room where I am happiest. Worries float up into a high ceiling so I can breathe, think of stars and small lives and rest through darkness into sunrise.

If matter is energy and we look into crevices, say, at my wrist until one cellular structure becomes distinct from another, one piece among many held in fluid interstices so the whole of me can go into the garden to harvest ripening tomatoes–

If we go smaller, beyond microscopic, and consider the space between the bits, how we are made not only of water but the emptiness inside atoms, and we are moving, not just pulse and blood or lymph and digestion or neurons firing but electrons rotating. We are quaking, cannot hold ourselves still.

Factor in time as illusion, an eternal unattainable present, only memory, hope and sorrow its boundaries. The heart aches before reaching the mountains. Light on water always follows the eye.

A high ceiling is a simple blessing, especially in summer, cool air, leaves visible through glass. Perpetual artifice of sky.

BEAUTY LAKE ON THE BEARTOOTH PLATEAU

Only a few clouds and breeze enough
to ripple the surface, light on every crest.

A whole lake of sparkling comes toward me,
and only a single fisherman down the shore.

Flat granite for a chair, a book, the risk
of staying too long and failing

to return to the car. I eat a red apple.
The fisherman disappears and the wind

comes down. Bears and mountain lions
live here. If the lake could speak–

What do you think the fisherman can't catch?

It would be easy to sleep in this sunshine
at the far end of a trail beside this large body.

How could you bear the loneliness if you stayed?

Light on water like fireflies in a field.
Focus on a spark and it's gone.

DO I ROMANTICIZE THE BEAR

Mist on the lake, a fact of air and water in September,
apple season, late chokecherry season. A grizzly
on the shore, no real surprise, its powerful ambling.

It wades in a few steps, lowers its snout to drink,
wanders through a dark cluster of pine then back to shore.
I want to go out but stay in the cabin's warmth. If I were

alone, I would venture—not enough to make fear
or danger—but to inhabit the same air, the same circle
of morning. What does it mean, this good,

good fortune to see a grizzly at dawn? And then
a single swan, its slow and dreamy paddle.

KELP FOREST, MONTEREY AQUARIUM

Small leopard shark, do we
lean into each other? Your eye

and my eye, my curiosity
and yours? And you, lovely rockfish.

I see how you turn to the sun,
to schools swirling above you

or how you collect, an audience
for these faces facing in.

Toddler watches me watching
anemones, watching tentacles,

and humans schooling
like anchovies.

Living sand dollars,
darling stars and jellyfish.

Small ray reaches up the side
of its tank like a puppy.

Humans must seem
like eccentric fish.

DOG SELF

Today I am lazy horizontal
can't keep my eyes open I want
a snack is someone going
somewhere can I come
I will sit and watch you
when you become boring
I will sleep and see your every
move don't think you can
get out that door without me

LATE SUMMER

Long time since a bird slammed
into my window, though it's the season.
Rowan berries are plump and birds
begin their feasting. This one, a robin,
falls flat on the porch then stands,
staggering, mouth open and panting.
Gradually his eyes brighten and
he looks almost ready to fly.
I return to my papers, my watcher
having watched the revival, until the bird's
cheeping startles me upward again.
Why haven't I considered the neighbor's cat?

My protector has fumbled, so my rescuer
runs to the locked door and knows
it will be too late. My coward
suppresses a knot in the belly and
turns her eyes away until the cat
disappears beyond the window frame,
bird in its jaw. Nature, I think.
No, a well-fed cat, says my ironist. And
my romantic, who has always clung
to the losses and wanted perfect
endings despite my editor's cutting
remarks, cries, *a poor robin gone.*

THE PRACTICE OF TREES

The yard would like to become a forest,
seedlings thick as grass. For a long time
I mowed and pulled, but they have
no regard for lawn and no limit—
ponderosa, spruce, linden, lilac, maple,
cherry, oak. A tricky lot, they shoot up
in secret and dig deep. Never mind
neighbors who keep weeds from cracks
in sidewalks and square-edge their lawns.
These stems have already hardened
into bark. Now, if I trim a branch
I fear pain in the severed limb. Mostly
I listen. When I ask what the trees want
the answer comes back: love us.

THE SELF CONSIDERS HER ALTERNATE SELVES

Who could live in other timelines, who were good at choosing, who were not so readily eased along or silenced.

The one who might have said, *I don't think so. No, this is not for me,* who then thought what *was* for her, how she could choose beyond what was offered, who might have gone away, at some point, far away, and who might still have come back.

Or the one who did not get away from the neighbor boy and who had little hope.

Or the one who took up singing because she was not afraid.

Or the sad one who could not get over being sad, who, when her colleague said this was navel gazing, said *which navel? Where?*

Or the one who didn't make it, one or another of the close calls—the car spinning on black ice, a sudden oncoming truck, a birth gone awry, or later propane, the one who ran to turn it off and went with the house into flames.

PRAIRIE WARBLER IN THE STREET

In the season of gumweed flowers
a bird perches on scrap iron before he
disappears into a hedgerow and sings.

Why does my mind flit to a quantum
image, an electron beginning in one place
then entering two open gates, its split self
traveling along corridors until one arrives
and cancels the other. I balance my
alternate futures, quick disappearance
or long life, equal and possible.

In certain moments, everything
becomes new. Light of summer in deep fall,
and today the bird, both memory
and a song inside leaves.

HUMAN PLOT

Worse when the waking comes earlier, sometimes hours
before sleep returns, and I read to pass the time. Last night,
a story about skin, how cortisol causes the microbiome

to alter, become gaunt, less able to inhabit and cultivate
the human surface, to produce collagen, ceramides,
acids and peptides—to balance and prevent the worst

bacteria from killing the others, to moisturize and keep
skin bright. No serum can compensate for stress-induced
loss. But what are they like, these creatures?

Do they burrow? Do they hide in the hilly landscape
of scars and oddities? I know only of those who live
on eyelashes, their almost-faces and six legs in magnified

photos, how they congregate invisibly, squeezing
into follicles. I learn that meditation, deep breathing
settles cortisol, makes us more suitable for habitation.

I inhale, massage my scalp, place hands over my face
as a healer might. *We are in this together,* I say, *now sleep.*

DOG BEACH

A woman whispers to her partner
she will not go barefoot, yet shoes
are useless against sea and sand.

In low tide, kelp and barnacle-covered
rocks, creatures kept wet in shadowy
interiors seem to rise into the air.

One scientist theorizes that when
we die, we don't leave but move on

to another layer of reality—some say
thirty-two or more folded like pastry.

Near a rock, I see what seems
like mussel shells crushed, but they are
clams making a broad swirl in sand.

A translucent blue crab circles
in the afternoon's small tide. I find
no dogs here, but there are many tracks.

IF I HAD SAID BEAUTY

My grown son and I
follow a prairie trail
leading to forest. Oblivious
to blooms in the early going,
he points as we begin
to climb.

Is that death
camas, he asks, and I say
yes. What's it good for,
he asks. *Death,* I say.
There must be something
else, he says. And I
don't reply.

Later,
the sun angles to create
eccentric shadow
and brilliance on a hill
covered in blossoms, each
a cluster, a spear.

THIS EMBRACE

One ponderosa leans inward where
        a slice of granite tips the trail as if
the tree compensates for the lurch,
        creates a curve to hold onto, and I do.

I feel something in my center, call it
        love for the younglings, the elders,
the twisted dead topping and edging the cliffs.
        Now, with you no longer ahead

on the trail, I hold to their steadiness
        and brace my weight.

EVENING SONG

I hardly know myself
and this has always been true.

Now I write the sun down
until the clanging voices stop.

Once light lifts from
the cliff and treetops,

the world contracts. Sky
closes in, and the singing starts.

That's when I hear
your voice again, my eyes

closed to shadows. You are
more than memory.

VOICES THROUGH WALLS

We are born into it, this silence
the deep history always obscure

voices we cannot hear
and there is wind, incessant wind

the yes and no of our days.
Now and then a sound comes

and we can hear its rhythms,
something close to words.

III

WHO ARE YOUR DEAD

If we became aware of the ancestral lives within us,
we might disintegrate.

–Carl Jung

1

Simple at first, half and
half. Then quarters, clear
enough, and more remotely, eighths,
and beyond that, almost invisible
except for the stories we keep–a patriarch
who nearly died fighting for the Union,
records from an old country, an elegant hand,
names. A farm. Simple.

2

Mother and her brother
searched and found, then quit
when a thief came along.

3

Double, double, until the mind stumbles,
a glimpse of the infinite
takes hold and all connection is possible.
Saints and assassins, hands turned
to their work. Ancestor against ancestor
in wars or petty dispute, and still

one from each side form a couple,
a lineage. A woman forced,
a love lost to a genealogical chart.
Secrets I can't get to.

4

The dead with their voices and stories
in languages I don't understand.
Who can say I am one thing, I am two?
So many strands, the dreams
and loathings of ancestors, accidental
and deliberate pairings churning in our cells.

OVER HOME

When we lived together, when my mother
and father, my brother and I still lived

in our house, my mother would say she was
going *over home,* meaning back to her parents,

to their two-story white farmhouse. Now,
when I dream of it, the roof opens to sky,

doors line a hallway and rooms hold
generations of treasures—stylish chairs,

strange musical instruments, disorderly
potential if only someone could keep it straight.

MY MOTHER'S ART ENTERS THE WORLD

Though I was sure my dolls' hair would
grow back when I trimmed, sure I could
see it extend into the air to confirm
what I already knew, I was left in these
later years with a collection of brutalized,
hard-sided, soft-sided, blonde and brunette,
multi-sized dolls who I don't remember
ever having loved—the more important
question always: what could I make them do?
I put them first in a plastic bag, then
in a Metropolitan Museum of Art bag
and let them sit in my office for months
while I lingered over an orange flowered
dress with gathered skirt, button back,
lace around its sleeveless openings, its model
a blonde with hair trimmed to the scalp.
I wondered if I should save the dress
my mother made, one more piece of her
handiwork, a diminishment, this
word, a sign of her skill and capacity to make
something out of raw material that fit
exactly this large-bodied doll and probably
matched a dress of my own. This morning
I walk the bag down four flights of stairs
to the Art Department Free Box
and think, now I will lose it, and then,
someone will find my mother's art.

YAHRZEIT, DECEMBER 1, 2020

for my mother

This year it's dry and warmish. I've been hiking
and feel confused by this odd season.
Ten years ago, wet flakes caked the streets
and though our morning visit was cut short
I planned to return to tell you about the storm.

Sundown, dishes done, a usual evening, I went
to bed and startled from sleep when the phone rang.
Why hadn't they called sooner, couldn't they see
you were leaving? Then I settled into your absence,
your body yours and not yours, the two of us
in your room, this shock of parting.

When I returned home I paced and the house
felt small, the ceiling too low, the hallway
narrow. I heard an engine outside, unmistakable
sound of trouble, and went out, 2 am, to find
a staggering young man, his car high-centered in snow.
I pushed, he worked the gas, we switched. Nothing.
Reeking of liquor, he abandoned the scene.

I stayed under the clear sky—its bluster long since
spilled—and walked, lumbered really,
through deep slush looking at stars. Exactly right:
the hemisphere of sky, distance, no confinement.
I walked and thought of you, how the impossible
had happened, and I tried to get used to it.

RETURN

In the morning I walk into the kitchen and look to the east. Sunrise over the small ridge, past machinery and the steep red grain bin my brother told me to climb once, to see if it was full, and then I slithered back down the roof to the waiting long ladder, grain bin my grandfather gave to my parents when they were married, its red peeling wood centered in the kitchen window.

It's odd that she's gone, odd the house still stands as though she just stepped out. I open the oven and find a potato she planned to bake and forgot. Its eyes have grown long and lapped the space twice, winding into the electrical units and rack, surviving for the past year and a half with no light.

Stillness everywhere, and dust. I thought I would be afraid of ghosts, of her ghost. As a child I ran down the hallway to my room and jumped under covers as though the thin layers would keep away any spirit, good or bad. I half-thought she would show herself and we'd have a conversation. She would complain, be confused about where she was or mad that she had left too soon, and I would reassure her, tell her I would clean up the mess, manage an orderly and respectful transition of her things into new hands. I would remember and love her.

I imagined there would be time to ask just a few more questions: who made the quilt she had stored in the cedar chest–could she please tell me once more–who was the young man who wrote to her from North Africa, how is Dad doing after all these years? Freed from the final mess, she would dispense words of advice, tell me what to do next, and for once I would listen.

A KIND OF TRUTH

A headwind through
    the bones.

My mother, long dead,
    let me know.

I remember the hike,
    the slight rise

in the trail, my son
    ahead,

suddenly I knew I didn't
    need to feel

more sorrow for her life
    or her death.

Get on with it,
    she said.

QUESTIONS

The new leaf asks the air,
        the step looks to the space ahead.
The pen queries the page, eyes interrogate
        the day. Isn't a kiss a question?
Yes? No? Those lucky ones who believe
        the answers, who speak as if
answers were absolute. Where does the line
        begin? Where does it end? Those
diagrams from elementary school, arrows
        in both directions. Even
the breadth of the line divisible,
        a world of questions.

SEWING ROOM, 1973

In the hot back room meant to be
a dressing room, as if dressing
should be set apart, there were two
oak chests full of treasures, letters
and jewelry, and a heavy sewing machine,
ancient and, according to my mother,

never quite right. I sat there
on hot summer days, light pounding
from curtainless windows, AM radio
tuned to Gladys Knight and the Pips,
Motown hits, and Diana Ross,
the most beautiful woman ever,

and I made school dresses in bright
polyester, the subtle smell of sewing
machine oil an undertow, me in my tank top
and shorts, a sweaty kid taking destiny
in hand, dreaming up a future to the whir
of the open belt and chuffing needle.

THINGS WILL OUTLAST

When a button comes loose from a heavy
wool coat, a union tag sewn alongside
weighty satin lining, I open a drawer
on my grandmother's sewing cabinet
and choose black thread from a decades-old
wooden spool, its label still adhering,
J & P Coats Best Six Cord, which will last
decades more for mending my own clothes
and the clothes of grown children and
maybe their children if people still
mend clothes. I sew the button in place
and wear this coat, my mother's from her
mid-century life, into a below zero world.

PROXIMITY TO FIRE

Fire warms a chilly room, a comfort
ancient and ordinary. In Norway,

the cousins say *cozy*, their homes carefully
considered, records of ancestors,

a chair my grandfather built
at fifteen before he left for America.

How lucky to sit quietly
in this hour before light floods the room.

I am on one side, the fire contained
on the other. In a moment I will

go to it, sit with my back to the flames,
a luxury, knowing I will not burn.

AFTER A MORNING SHOWER

I stand before a mirror buttoning my blouse
and watch my hands navigate downward
over blue disks sewn with yellow thread,
over the traits of women and men who
have made me to stand in morning steam,
one sum of their intentions. I have memorized
what photos appear in an old album,
their dark dresses, open faces. The women
wore earrings as I do, remained still
and unsmiling for the image to set.
What comes down or disappears could
be chance, my code put into play by
their codes. Even the air is an inheritance
from their world and the world before.

THIS MUCH

When my great great grandmother, whose name
I have just learned, was born March 25, 1839,
who was married June 28, 1863,
she did not know she would die one day short of her 49th
anniversary in 1912 having birthed 12 children in the Arctic
Circle, one of whom was my great grandfather
who would fall to his death in Seattle from a skyscraper's
scaffolding. She was named in the customary
way–Jensdatter–after her father, Jens
Pedersen. Her mother was named Eriksdatter,
and so it goes backward, the children named
after their father's first name, inscrutable,
less traceable in a linear, surnamed world. She was
Emilia Johanna, namesake to my grandmother, whose mother,
Andrea Kristofa Jorgensdatter died six months
after my grandmother was born. These women
with their mild expressions, broad foreheads, nearly forgotten
except for one-time portraits, old age images
from traveling photographers, and the dates and names
I hold to thinking I know this much.

FAMILY LETTERS

1

Terrible dry and we can't help it any.
Lethe has flowers planted. I'll not try
to tell you what they are for I don't know
how to spell the name. I hope you are still
in the notion of coming this winter
to California. I am so glad
you are getting your house fix(ed) so nice.
My Love to *all* and write when you can
Lethe has to read my letters now.
It rained over the mountains.
But that is not here.

2

Wish I could be with you
this Christmas. Will be
with Lethe and family. I am
wondering / wishing
that you will come sometime
this winter we are having
all kinds of weather.

THESE DARK DAYS

I leaf through my great grandmother's
photo album. On the last page,
her grandfather, my great, great, great–
handsome in his early middle age
and she a girl of eight or nine
with no idea she, Lizzy, will find her
Alonzo, and marry. They will have
three children and suddenly, when
the youngest is only six months old
she will die, something she ate.

My grandmother, oldest girl,
will quit school because she has
younger siblings, and when she
comes to Montana, she will bring
Emerson, her Latin, her mother's
photo album, not knowing I will
open its metal clasp, its velvet cover
on dark days leading to winter, and
search these faces to see who I am.

SHADE

Each time it is a thrill
to see my father, he comes
so seldom. Last night I caught
a glimpse through a café window
and lingered despite my fruitless
rushing in streets I did not
understand. He was there as
himself, not for me, as if he
just happened in, had not yet
seated himself, was simply
standing with his hat in hand,
wearing his jean shirt with its
practical breast pockets, taking
his time. When I looked through
the window he looked back.
I don't know if we spoke.

THE ONLY WORLD

The last time my father
carries me from the car
to the house I must be
six, maybe seven. Heavy
darkness curls around
us in the dirt and gravel
leading to the house.
I want to be still and
sleep. My brother
must be on the other
side of the back seat
and does my mother
carry him, since he
is smaller? I feel
a light jostle, my arms
around my father's
neck, my relief to be
lifted. Overhead
I feel but do not see
the cottonwood's massive
limbs, my head
on his shoulder, for
the moment he is
the center of the only
world I know.

LEGACY

Ripples on the pond, this splayed willow
a bouquet of branches. Insects and doves,
the conversation of white-billed ducks
practicing for the long way ahead. Red-winged
blackbirds trill from dead sentinel trees.

Before my father died, he and I spent
a day alone in the house. I watched him
do bicep curls with an old spring device,
all the rage in the 60s. I didn't know what
to think of his frailty. We talked about
keeping his strength up. He said
he always thought he would have more.

Money, he meant, but he could have
meant time. Blue dragonflies hover
in grass he must have planted, finches
shelter in cattails I seeded one summer
on this pond he made. Swallows dart
and dip, part of the conversation.

AUTOBIOGRAPHY OF THE SELF

A friend says my masculine side is well-developed,
meaning I can earn a living, be strategic, invest, lift
weights, same as any woman. Animus, she means.

In my twenties I learned Tai Chi, learned to trust
the Tan Tien drawing me as if through waist-high
water. I learned to yield, step aside and let the opponent

push through, and when the imaginary other began
to retreat I could advance. Later, I read Jung in earnest.
Too much self, a man told me. Selfish, he said.

In Jung's *Red Book*, you can see his journey
to the center and back, his pursuit, his art,
his return. When the aggressor retreats it is time

to move. The shadow, Jung says, is never gone,
even when it is obscured. Best to face the darkness
we walk with, Tan Tien drawing us along.

MID-AFTERNOON

for Philip

Each day we hike into wildness edging the city. Trails
wind and converge. Humans follow deer paths,
deer step over human prints. Ants migrate through sage
and sand which allows them to make their own
small city each spring.

Gnarled and twisted pines mark the way, their roots
surrounded by stone. Tree bodies choose to lie down
or lean into each other. In one place a hawthorn, its ripe berries
hanging in dark clusters, nearby a ponderosa where a single
magpie watches.

I love each step, the influx, the way boulders split
into uneven pieces when a juniper seeds itself on top.
And when we return home, the mountain ash, the last to let go
its leaves this fall, even on cloudy days, seems to
glow from within.

ACKNOWLEDGMENTS

My gratitude to the following publications in which these poems first appeared:

American Journal of Poetry: "Proximity of Fire" and "Dog Self"
Ascent: "Scene: Late Summer," "Kelp Forest," and "Sewing Room 1973"
basalt: "Do I Romanticize the Bear" and "Visitation"
Cutthroat: "Beauty Lake on the Beartooth Plateau"
Dark Matter: Women Witnessing: "Understanding Silence"
december: "These Dark Days," "Autobiography of the Self," and "Yahrzeit"
Facing Goodbye: "Ordinary Day"
Fugue: "The Edge of Things" and "Entanglement"
The Half-Life of Echoes: Poems about the Power and Fragility of Memories: "Voices through Walls"
Journal of Baha'i Studies: "A Kind of Truth" and "Legacy"
MicroLit Almanac: "Flicker Builds a Nest"
One Art: "Dog Beach," "Bat at Noon," "Over Home," and "What to Call This Embrace"
South Dakota Review: "How Light Disperses"
A Tribute To Ted Kooser: "Sewing Room 1973"
We Are All God's Poems: "Mid-Afternoon"
Welcome to the Resistance: "The Practice of Trees"

Special thanks to Melissa Kwasny and Mark Spragg for their detailed comments and deliberation over the collection. Thanks to Sheila Black, Cara Chamberlain, Danell Jones, Jim Peterson, Julie Schultz, Connie Voisine, and Joni Wallace for valuable feedback on individual poems. Thanks to the Newsletter Poetry Crew—John Reinhard, Diane Jarvenpa, Kirsten Crohn-Mills, John Straley, Meridian Johnson, John Terry, Richard Robbins, Timothy Murphrey and many other members over the years—for first glance at some of these poems in our monthly, decades-long sharing of work. Thanks also to Rachel and Deb Schaffer, colleagues and twin linguists at Montana State University Billings, who have answered questions about the odd twists of language that appear sometimes in these poems. My gratitude to MSU Billings for travel and residency support. Thanks also to Montana Artist Refuge, the Beartooth Wilderness Residency Program, and the Fine Arts Work Center for space to develop these poems and consider the possibility of this book.

Thanks to Christine Holbert and Lost Horse Press for believing in me and bringing this poetry collection into the world.

And to my family, deep gratitude for this journey we share.

The title for "The Edge of Things" is borrowed from Federico Garcia Lorca, "Theory and Function of the Duende."

"The Mind Lays by Its Trouble" is borrowed from Wallace Stevens, "Credences of Summer," line 5.

The inscription for "Who Are Your Dead," is taken from Carl Jung's *Notes on the Seminar in Analytical Psychology Given in 1925.*

"Family Letters" is a found poem excerpted and edited from Eliza Mason Han Johnson's letters.

"Autobiography of the Self" references Carl Jung's *The Red Book: Liber Novus*, New York: Norton, 2009.